US Department of
Transportation
**Research and
Special Programs
Administration**

Gettysburg National Military Park
Alternative Transportation System Planning Study

Final Report

June 2004

Prepared for:
National Park Service
Northeast Region
200 Chestnut Street
Philadelphia, PA 19106

Prepared by:
John A. Volpe
National Transportation
Systems Center
Kendall Square
Cambridge, MA 02142

REPORT DOCUMENTATION PAGE		Form Approved OMB No. 0704-0188

The public reporting burden for this collection of information is estimated to average 1 hour per response, including the time for reviewing instructions, searching existing data sources, gathering and maintaining the data needed, and completing and reviewing the collection of information. Send comments regarding this burden estimate or any other aspect of this collection of information, including suggestions for reducing the burden, to Department of Defense, Washington Headquarters Services, Directorate for Information Operations and Reports (0704-0188), 1215 Jefferson Davis Highway, Suite 1204, Arlington, VA 22202-4302. Respondents should be aware that notwithstanding any other provision of law, no person shall be subject to any penalty for failing to comply with a collection of information if it does not display a currently valid OMB control number.
PLEASE DO NOT RETURN YOUR FORM TO THE ABOVE ADDRESS.

1. REPORT DATE (DD-MM-YYYY) 06/2004	2. REPORT TYPE Planning Study	3. DATES COVERED (From - To) NA
4. TITLE AND SUBTITLE Gettysburg National Military Park Alternative Transportation System Planning Study		5a. CONTRACT NUMBER NA
		5b. GRANT NUMBER NA
		5c. PROGRAM ELEMENT NUMBER NA
6. AUTHOR(S) Volpe National Transportation Systems Center with Cambridge Systematics		5d. PROJECT NUMBER PMIS 56085
		5e. TASK NUMBER NPS TIC No. D-160
		5f. WORK UNIT NUMBER NA
7. PERFORMING ORGANIZATION NAME(S) AND ADDRESS(ES) U.S. Department of Transportation Research and Special Programs Administration John A. Volpe National Transportation Systems Center		8. PERFORMING ORGANIZATION REPORT NUMBER NA
9. SPONSORING/MONITORING AGENCY NAME(S) AND ADDRESS(ES) National Park Service Alternative Transportation Program 1201 Eye St. NW Washington, DC 20005		10. SPONSOR/MONITOR'S ACRONYM(S) WASO/ATP
		11. SPONSOR/MONITOR'S REPORT NUMBER(S) (see 5d. and 5e. above)

12. DISTRIBUTION/AVAILABILITY STATEMENT
Public distribution/availability.

13. SUPPLEMENTARY NOTES
This report addresses alternative transportation decision factors as indicated below (Y/N/NA):
(N) Non-construction options; (N) park carrying capacity; (Y) life-cycle/ops. & maintenance costs; (Y) cost-effectiveness.

14. ABSTRACT
This project identifies and evaluates transit service alternatives in the Gettysburg, Pennsylvania area, including Gettysburg National Military Park, the Borough of Gettysburg, and surrounding townships. The report concludes that public transit would allay the problems of resource damage due to traffic congestion and off-road parking, which would lead to enhanced visitor experience. Based on discussions with park service personnel and analysis of park visitation data, Volpe recommends a time frame to utilize a transit network during the peak-demand season. Finally, recommendations are made as to which vehicles should be purchased, how the added operations and maintenance costs should be funded, and the best method of service delivery.

15. SUBJECT TERMS
Gettysburg National Military Park, Alternative Transportation Program, Bus, Transit, Vehicle Selection

16. SECURITY CLASSIFICATION OF:			17. LIMITATION OF ABSTRACT	18. NUMBER OF PAGES	19a. NAME OF RESPONSIBLE PERSON Gary T. Ritter
a. REPORT None	b. ABSTRACT None	c. THIS PAGE None	NA	30	19b. TELEPHONE NUMBER (Include area code) 617-494-2716, ritter@volpe.dot.gov

Standard Form 298 (Rev. 8/98)
Prescribed by ANSI Std. Z39.18

Table of Contents

1.0	Executive Summary	3
2.0	Background	8
3.0	Existing Transit Services	13
4.0	Transit Alternatives	16
4.1	Overview	16
4.2	Common Elements	16
4.3	System Alternatives	17
5.0	Implementation Issues	27
5.1	Funding	27
5.2	Implementation Responsibility and Oversight	28
5.3	Method of Service Delivery	29
5.4	Vehicle Procurement	29
5.5	Operations and Maintenance Funding	29
5.6	Marketing and Promotion	30

List of Tables

Page

4.1   Summary Table of Gettysburg Transit Study Alternatives   26

List of Figures

2.1   Borough of Gettysburg and Gettysburg National Military Park   9

2.2   Automobile-Related Resource Damage on South Confederate Avenue   10

2.3   Historic Baltimore Street   12

2.4   Pedestrians Crossing U.S. Route 30 near Lincoln Square   12

3.1   Map of Existing Gettysburg Trolley Service   14

3.2   Trolley Operating in Lincoln Square   15

4.1   Transit Alternative 1 Route System   18

4.2   Parking along Hancock Avenue   19

4.3   Transit Alternative 2 Route System   20

4.4   Transit Alternative 3 – Park Loop System   23

4.5   Outlet Mall Complex Construction at Route 97 and Route 15   24

4.6   Transit Alternative 3 – Expanded Town System   25

1.0 Executive Summary

The purpose of this Alternative Transportation System Study is to define and evaluate alternatives for providing public transit service to the Gettysburg, PA area, including the Gettysburg National Military Park (GNMP), the Borough of Gettysburg, Cumberland Township and other surrounding townships. A number of factors have led to increased interest in implementation of public transit in this area, including:

- The General Management Plan (GMP) recently adopted for the GNMP calls for development of a new Visitor Center through a public-private partnership. The new Visitor Center will be located near Hunt Avenue, about one-quarter-mile southeast of the existing Visitor Center. The GMP identified a need for public transit to link the new Visitor Center with downtown Gettysburg borough and the more heavily visited battlefield sites.

- Resource damage resulting from traffic congestion and off-road parking is evident at some of the key attractions of the battlefield, including popular locations such as Little Round Top, Devil's Den, the Wheatfield and the High Water Mark. Park management supports public transit as a means of reducing automobile-related resource impacts, particularly during periods when demand for roadway and parking space exceeds capacity.

- There are a number of initiatives underway to attract additional visitors to the Borough of Gettysburg. These include the Gettysburg Pathways program, which is an initiative designed to preserve and interpret the Town's history and enhance the visitor experience in the borough. In addition to the Borough of Gettysburg, the Adams County Area Chamber of Commerce, the Gettysburg Area Retail Merchants Association, Gettysburg College, the Gettysburg Convention and Visitors Bureau, the GNMP Advisory Commission, the Lutheran Theological Seminary at Gettysburg, Main Street Gettysburg Inc., the Pennsylvania Department of Conservation and Natural Resources and the Pennsylvania Historical and Museum Commission are key participants in plans to develop the Gettysburg area. Numerous wayside exhibits that provide information on the borough's history and its role in the battle are in place as a result of this initiative. A separate partnership has resulted in a draft interpretive plan for the Borough of Gettysburg that was finalized in fall 2000. Public transit service between the Park and downtown Gettysburg has been identified as an important component in attracting visitors to downtown Gettysburg and interpreting the borough's important role in the battle and its aftermath.

- The Borough of Gettysburg and the GNMP are located in Adams County, which is one of Pennsylvania's fastest growing counties. The estimated 1995 population of just over 85,000 represents an increase from 57,000 in 1970 and 68,000 in 1980; rates of growth that far exceed those experienced statewide in Pennsylvania. Population is projected to exceed 100,000 by 2010. As a result, road congestion is an increasing problem, particularly along Route 30, which carries large volumes of commercial traffic through the center of Gettysburg. PennDOT is currently funding the Comprehensive Roadway Improvement Study (CRIS), which is designed to address current and future mobility problems in Adams County. This study is being coordinated with CRIS so that opportunities to address mobility problems with public transit are identified.

Three general alternatives for implementing public transit service in the Gettysburg area have been identified as part of this study. These alternatives were developed based on discussions with Park personnel, Borough officials and other public and private officials in the area, using established transit planning methods. The alternatives range from a basic system that meets immediate needs to a more extensive system that serves most major activity centers in the immediate Gettysburg area.

Based on a review of park visitation data, it is proposed that service be provided for seven months of the year, between April 1st and October 31st. Four levels of service would be provided, based on visitation levels. Service periods are defined below from period of highest service to lowest:

1. May 1st through Labor Day Weekend: Friday through Sunday;

2. May 1st through Labor Day Weekend: Monday through Thursday;

3. April 1st through April 30th and September 1st through October 31st: Friday through Sunday; and

4. April 1st through April 30th and September 1st through October 31st: Monday through Thursday.

Brief descriptions of the three proposed alternatives are provided below, while more detailed descriptions and maps are provided in the body of the report.

- **Alternative 1 (Minimum Option)** – This alternative includes two routes which would be timed to meet at the Park Visitor Center. The Park Loop would begin at the Visitor Center and provide regular service to Devil's Den, Little Round Top and the major attractions along Hancock Avenue. The Borough loop would provide service to the National Cemetery and Taneytown Road and then would proceed to Lincoln Square and the Lincoln Train Station using Baltimore Street for the trip into Gettysburg and Washington Street and Steinwehr Avenue for the return trip. Five vehicles will be required to service this option during peak periods. Therefore, estimated capital equipment costs are $1.7 million and estimated annual operations and maintenance costs are $425,000.

- **Alternative 2 (Enhanced Option)** – This option increases the geographic coverage provided under Alternative 1. Within the Park, coverage is expanded to provide direct service to the Wheatfield, as well as the Peach Orchard and Plum Run. In the Borough of Gettysburg, service is extended to Gettysburg College and the Lutheran Seminary. Eight vehicles will be required to service this option during peak periods.

The estimated capital equipment costs are $2.7 million and estimated annual operations and maintenance costs are $690,000.

- **Alternative 3 (Full Option)** – This option increases the geographic coverage provided under Alternative 2. Within the Park an additional loop is added connecting the Lutheran Seminary with West Confederate Avenue and Warfield Ridge. Another new route is added connecting the Visitor Center and downtown Gettysburg with the commercial area along Route 30 in Straban Township and the new Outlet Mall being developed at the Route 15/97 interchange in Mt. Joy Township. This route would run east along Route 30 to its interchange with the Route 15 Bypass. Ten vehicles will be required to service this option during peak periods. Therefore, estimated capital equipment costs are $3.4 million and estimated annual operations and maintenance costs are $890,000.

The selection and implementation of a preferred alternative requires that a number of factors be evaluated using both quantitative and qualitative criteria. The evaluation of these factors is beyond the scope of this study, but has been proposed as a Phase II follow-on study. Some of the key issues are summarized below:

- **Funding** – Potential sources of public and private funding need to be identified. If the desired alternative cannot be funded immediately, opportunities for the phasing in of service implementation need to be evaluated. Opportunities for offsetting costs through fares, advertising, public/private partnerships and other sources also need to be evaluated. Initial analysis indicates that fare revenue could help to offset a portion of operating costs, but any fare structure will need to accommodate group and family travel in an economical manner. All urban transit systems in the United States require operating capital grants from the Federal Transit Administration, as fare box revenues do not come close to sustaining operations.

- **Implementation Responsibility and Oversight** – Public transit service in the Gettysburg area is currently limited. The NPS contracts with Gettysburg Tours to provide service to the Eisenhower National Historic Site and private bus tours of the battlefield are offered along with an historic trolley service. The Adams County Transit Authority currently provides demand-responsive service to residents of the County, and has experience in operating service and handling the demands of State and Federal transit programs. In addition to the Transit Authority, options for oversight include existing public entities such as Adams County, the Borough of Gettysburg or GNMP, existing non-profits, such as Main Street Gettysburg, a new authority with representatives from existing agencies or an entirely new authority.

- **Vehicle Procurement** – In order for the new system to be successfully initiated and accepted as a viable means of accessing GNMP and Borough attractions, vehicles procured need to be reliable, comfortable and easily recognizable. Gettysburg Tours currently operates an historic, rubber-tired trolley service in Gettysburg and these vehicles fit well with the historic character of the area. While alternative fuel vehicles are desirable from an environmental standpoint, there are still concerns regarding reliability, availability of alternate fuels and maintenance. Capital costs are also higher than for gasoline or diesel vehicles. Since reliability and high recognition are the most critical components for success of a new system, it is recommended that gasoline- or diesel-powered historic trolleys be considered for initial purchase. Conversion to alternate fuel technology vehicles, such as liquefied petroleum gas (LPG, or propane) or compressed natural gas (CNG) can be undertaken following a successful introduction of the service.

- **Method of Service Delivery** – Service could be operated directly by a public agency or authority. However, since service is only needed initially for seven months of the year, contracting all or part of the operation and maintenance to a private operator is also a viable strategy. This latter method is most likely to provide the flexibility needed to adjust service levels based on demand. The NPS has successfully used private contracting to provide service to the Eisenhower NHS, where service levels are varied significantly over the course of the year. A mix of public and private operations may also be considered, especially if Alternatives 2 and 3 are ultimately implemented.

- **Operations and Maintenance Funding** – A number of Federal and State funding programs are available for capital equipment purchases but sources available to fund operations and maintenance are more limited. In order to sustain service over time, local sources of funding will need to be identified. Potential sources include fares, advertising, and contributions from local governments and local businesses. Coordination between all of these entities provides the best opportunities for sustained funding. Distribution of family or multi-day passes to visitors through hotels or local businesses is an example of a strategy that will involve multiple parties in funding of the system and encourage usage.

- **Marketing and Promotion** – Marketing and promotion of the system are critical to its success. While the new Visitor Center will serve as the focus of the promotional effort, it important that efforts be made to inform visitors of the availability of the system prior to their visit. Possible distribution channels include:

  – An extensive signage program on major routes;

  – Pennsylvania Welcome Centers;

  – Internet including cross-promotion with business sites;

  – Information included with hotel/motel reservations;

  – Press release and/or advertising in Civil War or tourist-related publications; and

  – Nearby tourist areas such as Lancaster and Washington, D.C.

2.0 Background

The Gettysburg National Military Park (GNMP) and the Borough of Gettysburg are nationally significant as the site of the Battle of Gettysburg, its aftermath and commemoration. At the beginning of the Civil War, the Borough of Gettysburg was a thriving county seat of English, German, Irish and African Americans of various religious, economic and cultural backgrounds. Like other communities across the nation, it reflected the political, social, and economic conditions typical of the period.

However, in July 1863, the town found itself at the center of the largest battle ever to take place on the continent. The armies of the Confederacy and the Union clashed on July 1, 2 and 3, 1863, in a battle that was the bloodiest in the history of the continent and one of the turning points of the American Civil War. While the great battle was being waged on the hills and in the fields surrounding the town, the residents endured Confederate occupation as prisoners of war. At the battle's end, they were left with the monumental task of caring for the thousands of wounded and burying the dead. In November 1863, President Lincoln focused the nation's attention on the cost, meaning, and consequences of the Civil War in his Gettysburg Address, and the battlefield's role in the remembrance of the battle was established.

Today, the GNMP surrounds the town (see Figure 2.1) and preserves and commemorates the sites of much of the significant battle action. Over 1.7 million visitors come to Gettysburg annually to learn about the events that took place there. Major destinations for visitors to the battlefield include: the Soldiers' National Cemetery, the site of Lincoln's Gettysburg Address; the park Visitor Center and Museum, including the Electric Map; the cyclorama painting of the battle; the Borough of Gettysburg, and its many battle and battle-related attractions; and numerous historic sites and monuments throughout the battlefield.

Surveys show that the most visited sites within GNMP are Little Round Top, the Eternal Peace Memorial, Confederate Avenue, and Hancock Avenue. The Eisenhower National Historic Site, the farm owned by the former president, is located adjacent to the southwestern boundary of the GNMP and is accessible to the public only by tour bus. Most visitor services, such as hotels, restaurants, and shopping, are located within the Borough of Gettysburg, Cumberland, and Straban townships.

The GNMP and the Borough of Gettysburg are located in Adams County in south central Pennsylvania. Adams County is primarily rural in nature but is located in close proximity to metropolitan areas, including York, Pennsylvania (20 miles), Harrisburg, Pennsylvania (37 miles), and Baltimore, Maryland (50 miles). The Park contains 5,989 acres of land and surrounds the Borough of Gettysburg (population 6,800) on three sides. Most of the Park is located within the boundaries of Cumberland Township, which is Adams County's second most populous municipality (population 5,800).

Figure 2.1 Borough of Gettysburg and Gettysburg National Military Park

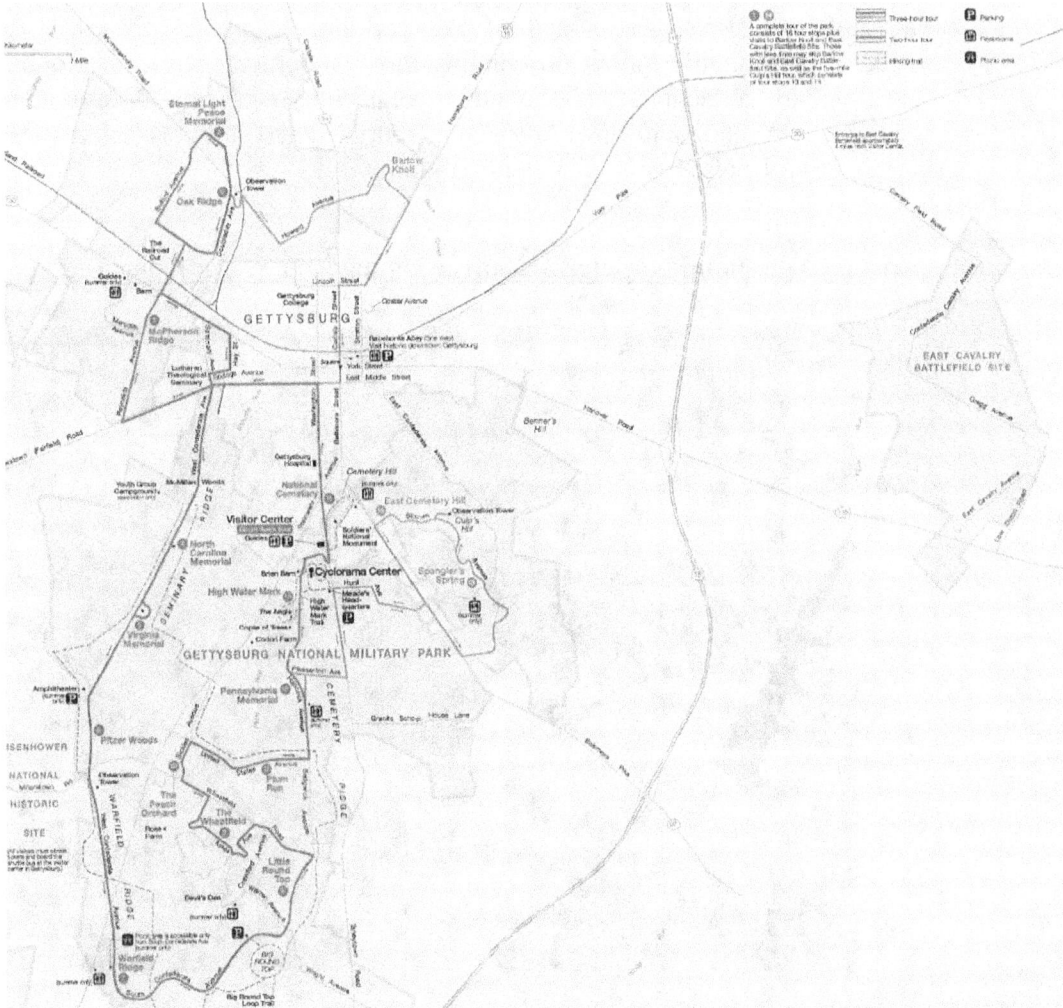

Several recent and ongoing initiatives have documented the transportation needs of the Gettysburg area and identified a need for public transportation. These initiatives include:

1. The **General Management Plan (GMP)** for the GNMP was adopted in the spring of 2000 after five years of development. The nationally preferred alternative calls for the development of a new complex for the Visitor Center, Cyclorama, limited retail and administrative functions to be located off Hunt Avenue between Baltimore Avenue and Taneytown Road, approximately one-quarter-mile southeast of the current location. An innovative financing plan has been developed for building this $40 million Center that will use a combination of concession revenue and private donations. In addition, the site of the current Visitor Center was the scene of significant activity during the battle and the NPS would like to restore the areas as close to its 1863 appearance as possible. One of the concerns expressed during the

public process was the increased distance between the Visitor Center and businesses that depend on the Park. These businesses are located primarily on Steinwehr Avenue and in downtown Gettysburg. Another concern is that automobile-related resource damage is occurring in heavily visited areas of the park (see Figure 2.2) as a result of traffic congestion and off-road parking. As a result, the GMP identified a need for two shuttle routes, one linking the Visitor Center to Little Round Top and nearby Park attractions and the other connecting with new Visitor Center with Steinwehr Avenue and downtown Gettysburg. These proposals form the basis of Alternative 1 presented in this memorandum.

Figure 2.2 Automobile-Related Resource Damage on S. Confederate Avenue

2. In 1999, the **Federal Lands Alternative Transportation Systems Study (ATS)** was initiated by the Federal Highway Administration (FHWA) and Federal Transit Administration (FTA) in cooperation with the National Park Service, the Bureau of Land Management and the U.S. Fish and Wildlife Service. The goal of the study was to estimate public transportation needs over the next 20 years for the three Federal Land Management Agencies involved in the study. Over 200 sites were evaluated, including the GNMP, and individual reports prepared for each site. The report prepared for the GNMP confirmed the needs identified in the GMP and also noted other opportunities for extending public transportation service in the future. In 2000, the National Park Service initiated an annual funding program for Alternative Transportation Systems, using $8.5 million from the FHWA Park Roads and Parkways Program. The ATS study includes a program development report that provides an outline for a Federal-aid program that would support ATS activities on and near federally owned and managed lands.

3. The **Gettysburg Pathways Plan** was developed in the early 1990s to increase visitation to the Borough of Gettysburg and educate those visitors on the role of the Borough in the battle. Stated goals were to preserve and interpret the Borough's history, and enhance the visitor experience in the area. In addition to the Borough of Gettysburg, Gettysburg College and Main Street Gettysburg, a local non-profit organization, are key participants. A series of wayside exhibits and walking tours were developed to help visitors understand the role of the Borough of Gettysburg in the battle. Major elements of the program still underway include improvements to the Steinwehr Avenue and Baltimore Street districts, expansion of transportation service and development of the Wills House, where President Lincoln finished writing his famous Gettysburg Address, into an interpretive facility. The Borough of Gettysburg is considering purchase of the Wills House. Other components include the rehabilitation of the historic Lincoln Train Station, where Lincoln arrived in Gettysburg, and the renovation of the College's Majestic Theatre. In all cases, the Borough wants to preserve historical sites and maintain the historical perspectives of the town, such as historic Baltimore Street, shown in Figure 2.3.

4. The **Gettysburg Interpretive Plan** was initiated in 1998 and was completed at the end of 2000. A Steering Committee was formed to guide the study which includes many of the same organizations involved in the Pathways Plan. The partnership includes the GNMP, the Borough of Gettysburg, the Adams County Area Chamber of Commerce, Gettysburg Area Retail Merchants Association, Gettysburg College, the Gettysburg Convention and Visitors Bureau, the GNMP Advisory Commission, the Lutheran Theological Seminary at Gettysburg, Main Street Gettysburg Inc., the Pennsylvania Department of Conservation and Natural Resources and the Pennsylvania Historical and Museum Commission. The goals and objectives of the Steering Committee are stated in the plan as: 1) interpret and educate for residents and visitors the role of the Borough in the battle, its aftermath and commemoration; 2) preserve resources; 3) benefit the residents of the Borough; and 4) maintain the quality of life. The Interpretive Plan builds upon the Pathways Plan to provide more detail on the role and function of the Train Station Welcome Center and the Wills House. The Plan also identifies the shuttle system as an integral part of the overall strategy. The shuttle would link the Visitor Center to the Borough, help to reduce automobile traffic and provide a return option to visitors who cannot walk the entire length of the expanded Pathway. The lead group for implementation of the Plan is Main Street Gettysburg, a community-based private non-profit group with a successful track record in the community.

5. The **Comprehensive Road Improvement Study (CRIS)** is being funded by the Pennsylvania Department of Transportation (PennDOT) with the goal of identifying existing and future deficiencies in the transportation system of Adams County and developing solutions. The study is focused on improving traffic flow within existing corridors, rather than on the development of new highway corridors. Within the immediate area of Gettysburg traffic concerns focus on U.S. Route 30, which carries large volumes of traffic through the historic center of the Borough. As part of this study, the GNMP requested that the CRIS efforts be monitored and that GNMP interests be represented in that process.

Figure 2.3 Historic Baltimore Street

The volume of traffic, and particularly the number of trucks, is of major concern to the Borough in its efforts to attract additional tourists. Traffic congestion and the difficult pedestrian environment (see Figure 2.4) both detract from the historic character of downtown Gettysburg. The CRIS study is looking at a variety of solutions to reduce the impact of this traffic on downtown Gettysburg, but still provide adequate mobility for a growing population and employment base. While CRIS is focused primarily on highway and traffic-oriented solutions, public transportation is also a potential part of the solution.

Figure 2.4 Pedestrians Crossing U.S. Route 30 near Lincoln Square

3.0 Existing Transit Services

The majority of visitors (more than 80%) to the GNMP use private automobiles to access the site and to travel along well-marked auto tour routes, in most cases using interpretive audio cassettes purchased at the Visitors Center. While there is no traditional fixed-route public transportation in Gettysburg, there are other transit services that do play key roles:

- Private tour buses carry a significant number of visitors into the Park, with greater numbers in the shoulder seasons in April, May, September and October. Some buses go to the Visitor Center and obtain a Licensed Battlefield Guide for their tours, while others either go to the Visitor Center and tour the battlefield on their own or go directly to the battlefield. The current visitor counting methodology is based on the assumption that about 55 percent of bus tours use the Center.

- Gettysburg Tours, a private company, provides guided tours of about two hours in length. The tours use a variety of buses and generally make one stop along the Battlefield at Little Round Top. Gettysburg Tours does not provide specific ridership information for this service but estimates that seven to eight percent of visitors to the GNMP take their guided bus tours. Additional service provided by Gettysburg Tours consists of one rubber tired trolley route linking the Visitor Center, destinations in the Borough of Gettysburg and motels along the Route 30 East commercial strip. Service is provided once per hour. The service was initiated in 1999 using two routes, but these were combined into a single route for 2000. The route map is shown in Figure 3.1.

    Most of the ridership for this service comes from unlimited ride tickets that are sold either at the company's terminal on Baltimore Street or in local lodging facilities. The trolleys can be used like a regular transit system and boarded for a $1.00 fare but the company reports that this represents a very small proportion of ridership. Trolley service is provided between April and October. Figure 3.2 shows typical operating conditions in Lincoln Square for the existing trolley service.

- The Eisenhower National Historic Site is only accessible by bus and guided tour. Buses run from the Visitor Center with service provided on a maximum of half-hour headways during the peak season to a minimum of four trips per day during the winter months. Adult fares for the bus ride and tour are $5.25; children's fares are either $3.25 or $2.25, depending on age. Gettysburg Tours runs this service under concession agreement, with the NPS receiving two percent of gross revenue. Both Park personnel and Gettysburg Tours note that visitation has been declining and that many visitors are over 65 years of age. The Eisenhower NHS drew 77,000 visitors in 1998, down from over 100,000 visitors in 1994.

- The Adams County Transit Authority (ACTA) operates demand responsive service in the County, primarily for elderly, low-income and disabled residents. This service is operated with small buses and primarily provides transportation to Gettysburg for medical, shopping and other trip purposes. There is also significant usage in the southeastern portion of the County near Hanover. The service is managed by Rabbit Transit of York County under a contract arrangement. The annual budget of ACTA is approximately $500,000. Funds come from a variety of transportation and human service programs. There is no traditional fixed route transit service in the County.

Figure 3.1 Map of Existing Gettysburg Trolley Service

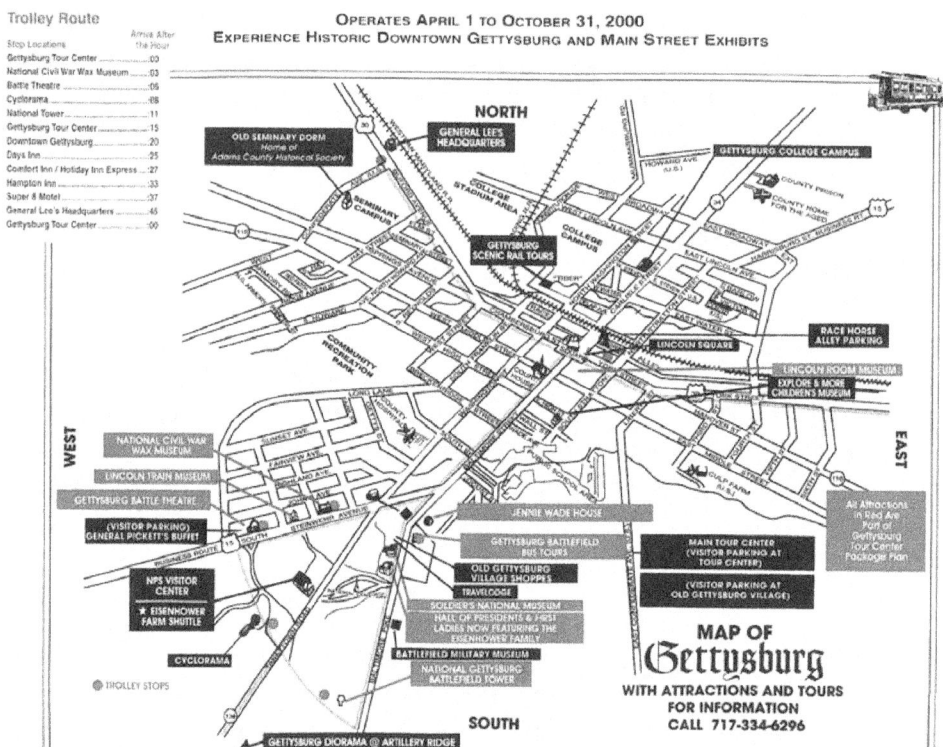

Source: Gettysburg Tours.

Figure 3.2 Trolley Operating in Lincoln Square

4.0 Transit Alternatives

4.1 Overview

Three system alternatives for transit service in the Gettysburg area are presented in this section. Alternative 1 is a basic system that meets the highest priorities of the Borough of Gettysburg and the National Park Service as defined in the GMP and other plans. These priorities are influenced primarily by the planning and economic development activities described in Section 2.0. Alternative 2 provides a minor expansion of the basic service within the GNMP and extends the Borough service north to Gettysburg College and west to the Lutheran Seminary. Alternative 3 adds a major extension of service within the Park that covers West Confederate Avenue, and adds a new route covering the commercial area along Route 30 East between downtown Gettysburg, the Route 15/Route 30 interchange, and the new Outlet Mall being constructed at the Route 15/Route 97 interchange.

These alternatives have been developed so that service can be phased in or expanded over time. If funding is only available initially for Alternative 1, then Alternatives 2 and 3 can be phased in later as funding becomes available. The alternatives described below are based on the assumption that the new Visitor Center near Hunt Avenue will be the "hub" or major transfer point for the system. However, if service is initiated prior to the opening of the Visitor Center, the parking lot of the existing Visitor Center could effectively serve the same purpose. It is also assumed that after opening of the new Visitor Center, access for transit vehicles will be maintained between Taneytown Road and Steinwehr Avenue somewhere in the vicinity of the current Visitor Center and Cyclorama. This access is described below as "existing driveway."

An important restriction on the development of all three alternatives is the fact that the streets and roads themselves are national landmarks, and cannot be altered in any way to accommodate transit vehicles.

4.2 Common Elements

The three alternatives described below all have common elements based on an analysis of visitor patterns:

- Service would be provided between April 1st and October 31st. Visitation drops off between November and March to a level where service probably cannot be economically justified. New attractions and employment opportunities being developed in the area may increase off-season visitation over time and generate more demand by local residents. The period of service could be extended gradually if this is the case.

- "Peak" months of service were defined as those with the highest level of visitation, May, June, July and August. Off-peak months are defined as April, September, and October. During both peak and off-peak months, a higher level of service would be provided on weekend days, which are defined as Friday, Saturday, and Sunday. Service levels were thus calculated for four separate time periods:

1. Peak months/weekend;
2. Peak months/weekday;
3. Off-peak months/weekend; and
4. Off-peak months/weekday.

- In order to provide the most efficient service possible to both the Borough and the GNMP, and to clearly communicate with the riding public, several "routes" may be identified. However, the equipment will be standardized, and the new Visitor Center will serve as the transfer point between all routes. Depending on the eventual expansion of the system, a transfer point my also be placed in Lincoln Square.

- For purposes of cost estimation hours of service are assumed to be 8:00 a.m. to 6:00 p.m. Service levels are varied throughout the day based on patterns of demand. All routes receive service at least once per hour; during peak periods service may be as frequent as every 10 minutes.

- It is assumed that historic trolleys seating 22 passengers will be used to provide the service. These vehicles will provide the maneuverability required to meet the proposed schedules. Additionally, all vehicles will be equipped to accommodate handicapped persons in accordance with the Americans with Disabilities Act (ADA).

- Cost estimates assume that vehicles would be high-quality diesel powered historic trolleys with some customized features. A cost of $300,000 per vehicle is assumed, as these will be Altoona-tested replica trolleys[1]. While less expensive vehicles of this type can be purchased it is important to minimize required maintenance funds over time. Operating costs include both a cost per mile, which primarily consists of fuel and parts, a cost per hour, which consists primarily of labor, and a fixed cost for management and administrative expenses. Unit costs were compared to those of several small transit properties in the region, including Altoona, Johnstown, and Williamsport in Pennsylvania, and Frederick and Hagerstown in Maryland.

4.3 System Alternatives

Alternative 1 provides a basic service between the Visitor Center and downtown Gettysburg and between the Visitor Center and Little Round Top. Access would also be provided to Devil's Den and the Wheatfield. Routes are shown graphically in Figure 4.1.

---

[1] The Federal Transit Administration requires that all production buses purchased using federal funds complete a rigorous bus testing program in Altoona, PA This test program covers durability, maintainability and many other key aspects of bus reliability

Figure 4.1 Transit Alternative 1 Route System

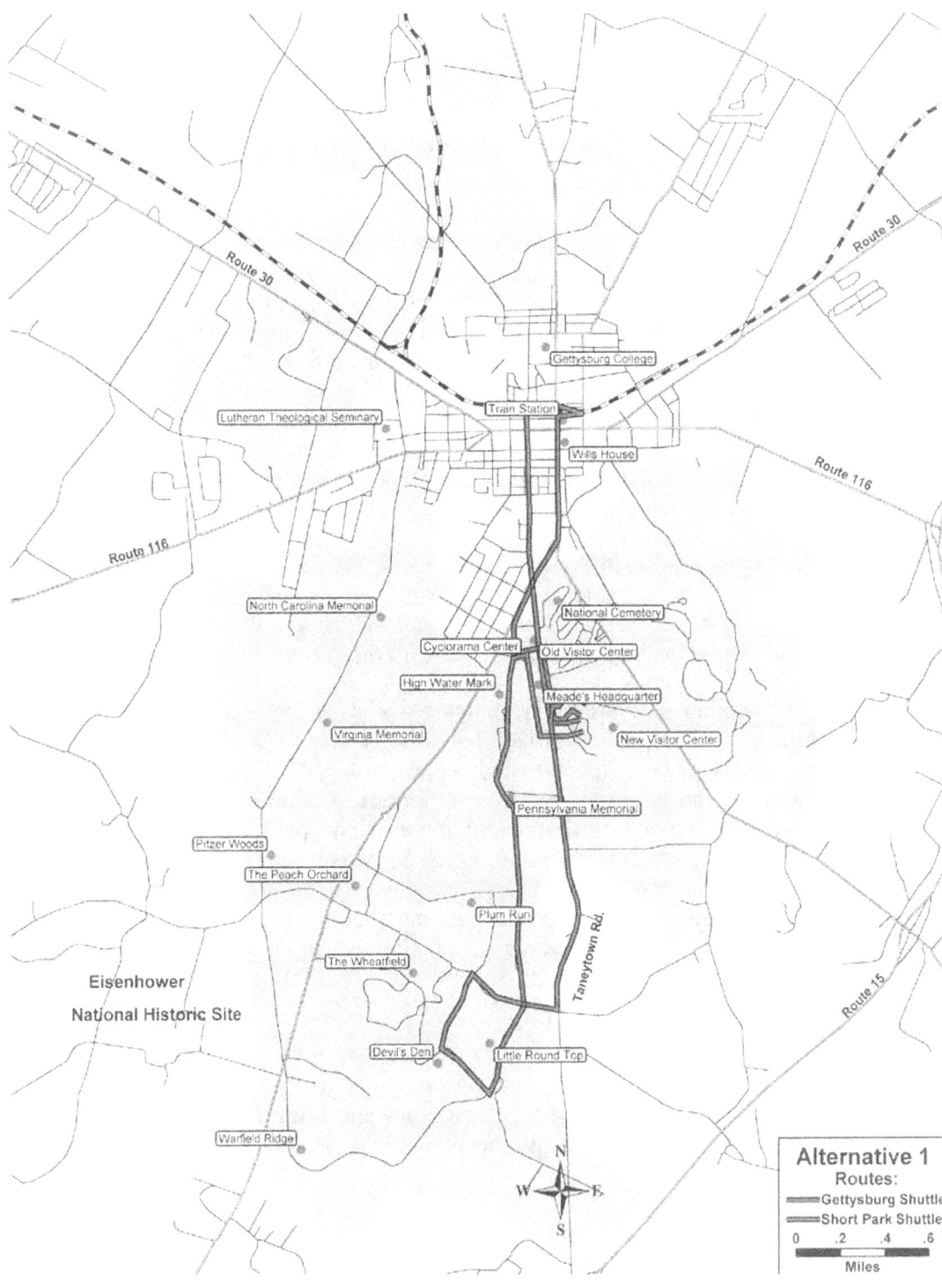

The **Borough loop** would leave the new Visitor Center, travel north on Taneytown Road, stop at the Soldier's National Cemetery, and continue to Baltimore Street, north on Baltimore to Lincoln Square, and then north on Carlisle Street to the Train Station. The route would continue from the Train Station westbound on Railroad Avenue and southbound on Washington Street to Steinwehr Avenue. The route would take Steinwehr Avenue south to the existing driveway, cross to Taneytown Road and then travel south to the Visitor Center entrance.

The **Park loop would** leave the Visitor Center and travel south on Taneytown Road to Wheatfield Road, where it would make a right turn. The route would then make a counterclockwise loop traveling west on Wheatfield Road, south on Crawford Avenue, east on Warren Avenue and north on Sedgwick Avenue to Little Round Top. The route would then continue north on Sedgwick and Hancock Avenues past the Pennsylvania Memorial, Angle and the High Water Mark. Figure 4.2 illustrates some of the parking conditions in the area. The route would then travel east on the existing driveway to Taneytown Road and return to the Visitor Center.

Figure 4.2 Parking along Hancock Avenue

The two loops included in this alternative would require five buses, with an estimated capital cost of $1.5 million. It is estimated that an additional 10 percent to 15 percent would be required for shelters, informational materials and other amenities. During most periods, buses on both loops would run every 15 minutes. During off-peak months on weekdays, frequency of service could be reduced to 30 minutes. Annual estimated costs for operations and maintenance are approximately $425,000.

Alternative 2 expands geographic coverage of both of the loops identified in Alternative 1 to serve additional destinations in both the Borough and the Park. Alternative 2 is shown graphically in Figure 4.3.

Figure 4.3 Transit Alternative 2 Route System

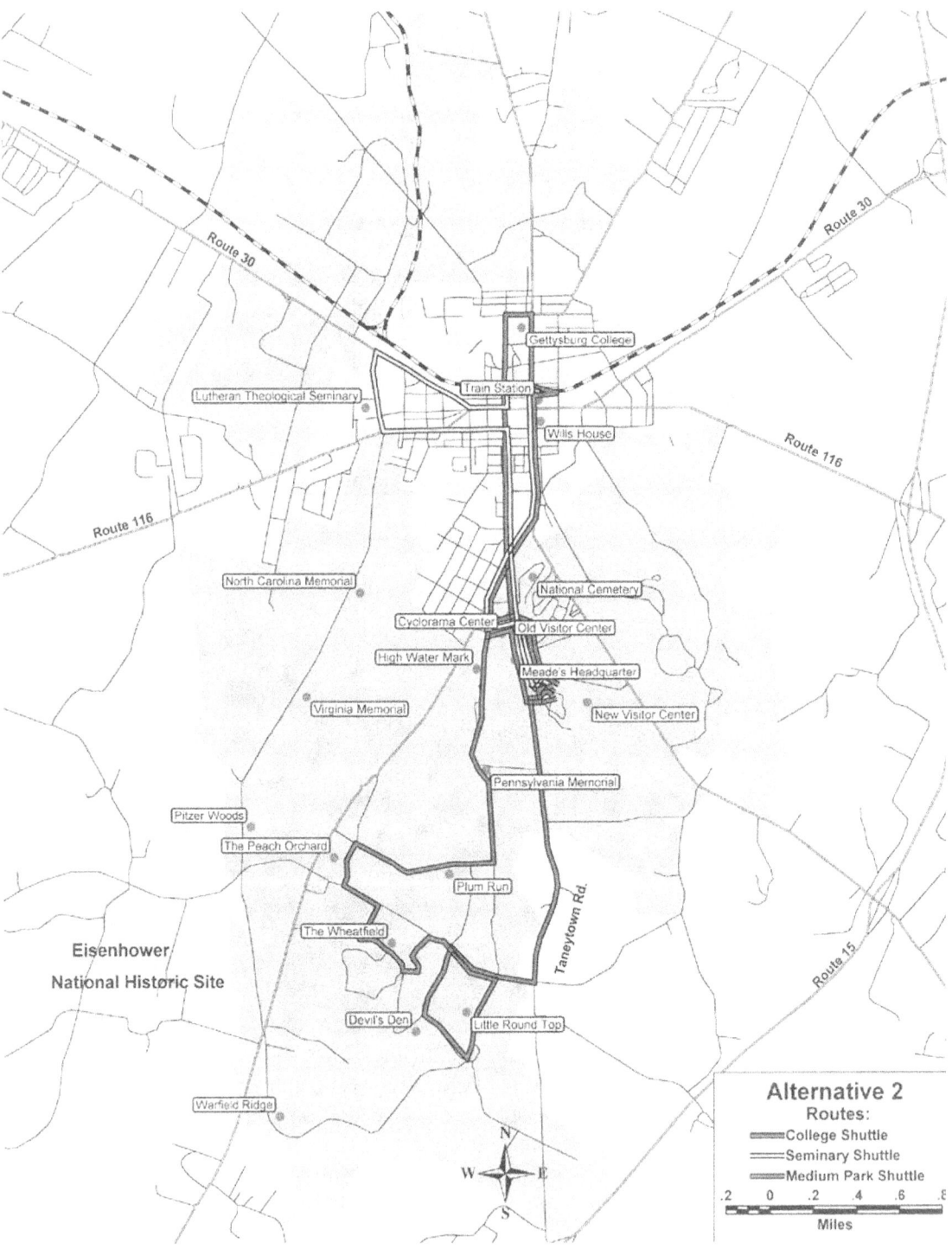

The **Borough loop,** which would be expanded to serve Gettysburg College and the Lutheran Seminary, could either be expanded to create one large loop, or split into two loops with one serving the College and the other serving the Seminary. An alternative showing two loops is presented below. However, combining the two loops into one would have minimal impact on cost and ridership.

The first loop, **Borough/College loop**, would follow the same path as Alternative 1 to the Lincoln Train Station (Visitor Center, Taneytown Road, National Cemetery, Baltimore Street, Lincoln Square, and Carlisle Street). The route would continue northbound on Carlisle Street to Lincoln Avenue, where it would turn west to serve the Gettysburg College campus. The College, which existed as Pennsylvania College at the time of the battle, is proposed to be a significant part of the Interpretive Plan. The service would also be available to service the needs of students and employees during the spring and fall months. The route would then turn southbound from Lincoln Avenue to Washington Street and continue to Steinwehr Avenue. The route would return to the Visitor Center via Steinwehr Avenue, the existing driveway and Taneytown Road.

The second loop, **Borough/Seminary loop**, would follow the same path as Alternative 1 and the Borough/College loop to the Lincoln Train Station. The route would then turn west onto Railroad Street and south onto Washington Street, continuing to U.S. Route 30 (Chambersburg Street). The loop would then travel west on Route 30 to the Lutheran Seminary. From there it would travel south on Seminary Ridge Avenue through the Seminary campus. The Seminary played an important role in the battle and is part of the auto tour. The route would then turn east onto Middle Street and then south on Washington Street to Steinwehr Avenue. It would then return to the Visitor Center in the same manner as the **Borough/College loop.**

The **Park Loop** would also be expanded to serve additional destinations in the south portion of the Park, including the Peach Orchard and Plum Run. The Wheatfield would receive more direct service than under Alternative 1. The Park loop would begin as in Alternative 1, traveling south on Taneytown Road to Wheatfield Road, and making the counterclockwise loop via Crawford, Warren and Sedgwick Avenues. After serving Little Round Top, the route would return to westbound Wheatfield Road and then loop behind the Wheatfield itself, using Ayres Avenue. After returning to Wheatfield Road, the route would continue westbound, then northbound onto Sickles Avenue, and eastbound onto United States Avenue. The route would then return to the Visitor Center as in Alternative 1, using Hancock Avenue, the existing driveway and Taneytown Road.

Alternative 2 would require a total of eight vehicles for a total capital cost of $2.4 million, with an additional 10 percent to 15 percent for amenities and other infrastructure. Each of the town loops would run every 30 minutes. Thus Steinwehr Avenue, the downtown area and the Train Station would be served every 15 minutes; the College and Seminary would be served every 30 minutes. The Park loop would run every 15 minutes except during the midday period on weekends when service would be required every 10 minutes. During off-peak weekdays, the frequency of service would be reduced to 20 minutes for the Park loop but remain the same for the College and Seminary loops. Annual estimated costs for operations and maintenance would be approximately $690,000.

Alternative 3 expands upon Alternative 2 to serve some of the growing traffic generators outside of the Park and the Borough of Gettysburg. This option provides service to growing retail and employment areas and would have a stronger chance of attracting local residents in addition to visitors. New areas served would be the Route 30 commercial area east of Gettysburg in Straban Township, and the Outlet Mall being developed at the Route 97/Route 15 interchange in Mount Joy Township.

Alternative 3 would maintain the routes identified in Alternative 2 and expand service to two new routes, one within the Park and one outside of the Park. The **new Park Loop** expands service to the popular visitor destinations along West Confederate Avenue. This route would travel from the Visitor Center to the Lincoln Train Station via Taneytown Road, Baltimore Street, Lincoln Square, and Carlisle Street. It would then travel the same route as the Borough/Seminary shuttle (Railroad Street, Washington Street, Route 30 West and Seminary Avenue) to Seminary Avenue and Middle Street. From there it would continue south onto West Confederate Avenue past the North Carolina and Virginia Memorials, to South Confederate Avenue, Sedgwick Avenue, Hancock Avenue, existing driveway, and Taneytown Road to the Visitor Center. The expanded Park loop system is shown in Figure 4.4.

Figure 4.4 Transit Alternative 3 – Park Loop System

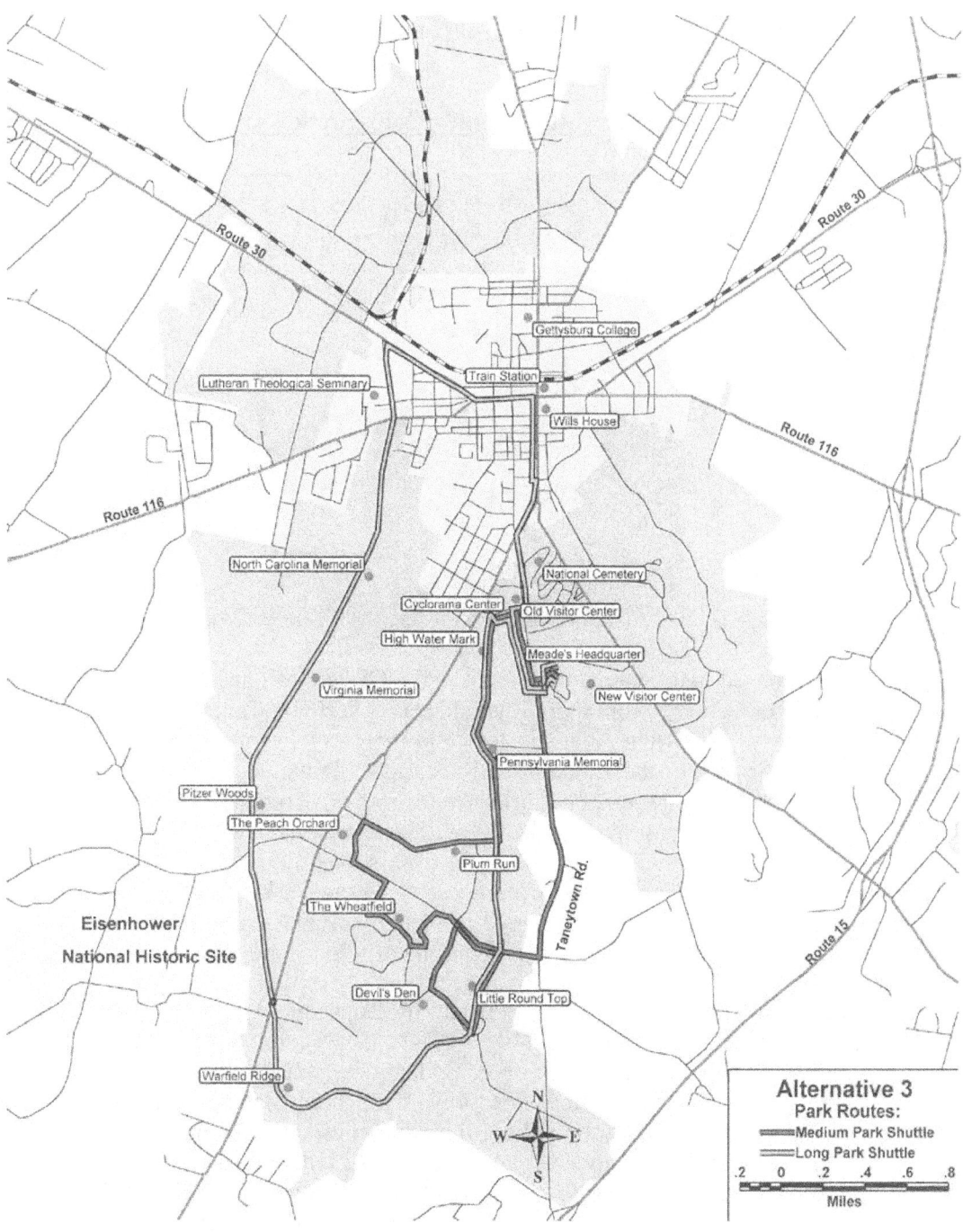

The new Route 30 shuttle would link the Visitor Center and downtown with the developing commercial and lodging area along Route 30, and with the new Outlet Mall complex under development at Route 97 and Route 30 (Figure 4.5).

Figure 4.5 Outlet Mall Complex Construction at Route 97 and Route 15

The proposed new route would begin at the Outlet Mall and travel north on Route 97 to the Visitor Center. From there it would travel north on Taneytown Road, to the existing driveway to Steinwehr Avenue. It would then travel north on Baltimore Street through Lincoln Square to the Lincoln Train Station. It would then leave the Lincoln Train Station and travel south on Carlisle and east on Route 30 (York Street). The route would continue east on Route 30 with the motels along the road as the primary destinations. Shopping areas could also be served on demand. The existing terminus would be at the Hampton Inn just west of Route 30 but if development occurs at the Route 15/Route 30 interchange as planned an extension may be warranted. The configuration of this route is shown graphically in Figure 4.6.

Due to the length of the new routes and the consequent high cost, the Route 30 shuttle and the expanded Park loop shuttle on West Confederate Avenue are both proposed for hourly service. Direct phone or computer connections should be installed in motels along Route 30 so that stops are only made upon demand and potential riders can receive real-time information about the next shuttle availability. These two new routes would expand the required vehicle fleet to 10, with an estimated capital cost of $3.0 million plus 10 percent to 15 percent for additional infrastructure and amenities. Annual operations and maintenance costs for this system is approximately $890,000.

The operating characteristics of the three alternatives are summarized in Table 4.1. Route lengths, travel times, headways and vehicle requirements are shown for each alternative and each route. It should be noted that these are estimates for costing purposes only and will require adjustment as a more detailed Phase II analysis is conducted.

Figure 4.6 Transit Alternative 3 – Expanded Town System

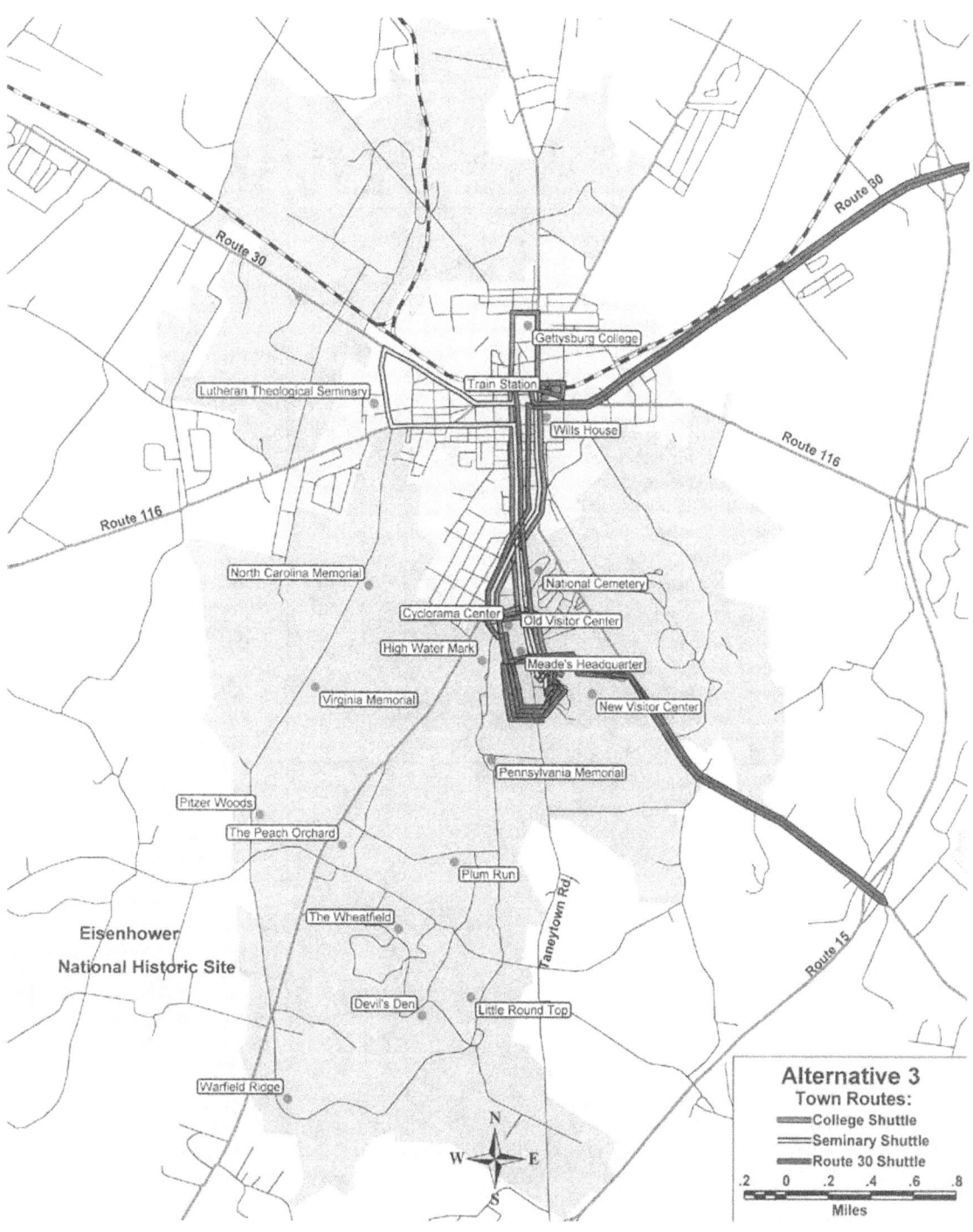

Table 4.1 Summary Table of Gettysburg Transit Study Alternatives

Route	Alternative #1		Alternative #2			Alternative #3 Additions**	
	Short Park Shuttle	Gettysburg Shuttle	Medium Park Shuttle	College Shuttle	Seminary Shuttle	Long Park Shuttle	Route 30 Shuttle
Length (miles)	5.2	3.8	6.9	4.5	5.3	9.7	10.5
Travel time (minutes)	18.5	19.0	23.0	22.5	26.0	32.0	45.0
Cycle time (minutes)*	30.0	29.0	40.0	35.0	40.0	54.0	59.0
Headways (Minutes Between Buses)							
Weekday – May through September							
Peak weekday before 12 noon	15	15	15	30	30	60	60
Peak weekday 12 noon to 2:00 p.m.	15	15	15	30	30	60	60
Peak weekday after 2:00 p.m.	15	15	15	30	30	60	60
Weekend – May through September							
Peak weekend before 12 noon	15	15	15	20	20	60	60
Peak weekend 12 noon to 2:00 p.m.	10	15	10	30	30	60	60
Peak weekend after 2:00 p.m.	15	15	15	20	20	60	60
Weekday – April, Sept., Oct.							
Off-peak weekday before 12 noon	30	30	20	30	30	60	60
Off-peak weekday 12 noon to 2:00 p.m.	30	30	20	30	30	60	60
Off-peak weekday after 2:00 p.m.	30	30	20	30	30	60	60
Weekend – April, Sept., Oct.							
Off-peak weekend before 12 noon	15	15	15	30	30	60	60
Off-peak weekend 12 noon to 2:00 p.m.	15	15	10	30	30	60	60
Off-peak weekend after 2:00 p.m.	15	15	15	30	30	60	60
Vehicles Needed on Route							
Weekday – May through September							
Peak weekday before 12 noon	2	2	3	2	2	1	1
Peak weekday 12 noon to 2:00 p.m.	2	2	3	2	2	1	1
Peak weekday after 2:00 p.m.	2	2	3	2	2	1	1
Weekend – May through September							
Peak weekend before 12 noon	2	2	3	2	2	1	1
Peak weekend 12 noon to 2:00 p.m.	3	2	4	2	2	1	1
Peak weekend after 2:00 p.m.	2	2	3	2	2	1	1
Weekday – April, Sept., Oct.							
Off-peak weekday before 12 noon	1	1	2	2	2	1	1
Off-peak weekday 12 noon to 2:00 p.m.	1	1	2	2	2	1	1
Off-peak weekday after 2:00 p.m.	1	1	2	2	2	1	1
Weekend – April, Sept., Oct.							
Off-peak weekend before 12 noon	2	2	3	2	2	1	1
Off-peak weekend 12 noon to 2:00 p.m.	2	2	4	2	2	1	1
Off-peak weekend after 2:00 p.m.	2	2	3	2	2	1	1
Vehicle requirement	5		8			10	
Vehicle capital cost	$1,500,000		$2,400,000			$3,000,000	
Other capital costs	$200,000		$300,000			$400,000	
Annual operations and maintenance cost	$425,000		$690,000			$890,000	

* Cycle time includes stops and layover at ends of route.
** Alternative 3 includes all elements of Alternative 2 – costs are for entire system, not just additions.

5.0 Implementation Issues

5.1 Funding

Potential sources of public and private funding for capital equipment and facilities need to be identified, and this is proposed as a task in Phase II. Public sources of funding are generally oriented toward purchase of capital equipment, but funds can be obtained from State and Federal sources for operating expenses. The recent formation of the Adams County Transportation Planning Organization (ACTPO) represents a significant change in the way that State and Federal transportation funds are distributed. Although Adams County is not an urbanized area ACTPO is parallel to the Metropolitan Planning Organizations required in urbanized areas by Federal law. ACTPO includes representatives of PennDOT, local boroughs and townships and other public agencies in the county. Its purpose is to set priorities for the expenditure of transportation funds in the County. This is significant because a number of the major funding programs under TEA-21 permit funds to be used flexibly for either highway or transit uses.

Specific funding programs include:

- The Federal Transit Administration (FTA) of the U.S. Department of Transportation is the primary Federal source used for purchase of public transportation equipment. Funds are provided to both State DOT's and directly to metropolitan areas of greater than 50,000. Adams County does not qualify for the latter category of funds and thus receives FTA funds through PennDOT. These funds are currently used to provide demand responsive service to elderly and disabled residents of the County. PennDOT distributes funds to non-urbanized areas through the Rural Public Transportation Program (Act 26 of 1991) for capital, operating and technical assistance.

- PennDOT also provides funds to non-urban systems through the Transit Capital Assistance Program, which provides for new equipment, major overhaul, and supporting infrastructure such as maintenance facilities. The Transit Research and Demonstration program is a competitive program that provides financial assistance for innovative projects that enhance the attractiveness of public transportation. Both programs require local matching funds.

- The FHWA provides funds to the National Park Service under the Park Roads and Parkways (PRP) Program. These funds are used primarily for roadway and parking projects but may be used for public transportation facilities as well. The NPS is currently setting aside approximately $8 to $9million annually for public transit projects serving National Parks. Service between Parks and gateway communities is eligible for funding, as well. With available funds so limited, competition for these funds is very intense. The funding level for this program, however, is likely to increase significantly in the future.

- Funds provided under other major FHWA programs, including the National Highway System (NHS) program, the Surface Transportation Program (STP) and

Transportation Enhancements (TE) permit funds to be shifted between highway and transit facilities. If support for implementation of a transit system can be obtained, ACTPO can work with PennDOT and FHWA to identify funding opportunities from these sources. It is also important to note that funds provided under the PRP program can be used as a match for other Federal transportation funds.

5.2 Implementation Responsibility and Oversight

Public transit service in the Gettysburg area is currently limited. The NPS contracts with Gettysburg Tours to provide service to the Eisenhower NHS and private bus tours of the battlefield are offered. The Adams County Transit Authority provides demand-responsive service to County residents, but its mission and resources are limited. It does, however, have experience in both operations and management of State and Federal transportation program funds. Options for oversight include:

- Adams County Transit Authority – The mission and board of the Transit Authority could be expanded to implement and provide oversight for the new services. The Authority's board would probably need to be expanded to accommodate those with a direct and indirect financial interest in the new system, including both public and private organizations. The Transit Authority is already empowered to receive Federal and State transit funds but the service as proposed would result in a significant change in its mission.

- A new authority could be formed specifically to operate the new system. The board would again include those with a direct and indirect financial interest in the service. Participants would include the Borough, the County, the NPS, the Museum Foundation, the Chamber of Commerce and the Convention and Visitors Bureau, among others. This authority would have to be empowered to receive public funds and thus create some redundancy, but it would have the advantage of being able to concentrate on a single mission.

- Oversight could be accomplished through existing municipalities with the Borough of Gettysburg and Adams County being the most likely candidates. Most of the area served by the Town routes would be within the Borough and much of the needed support could probably be provided by existing departments and personnel.

- The Park could also provide oversight of the service, similar to the system now in place in Acadia National Park. Memoranda of understanding would be required for the Park to provide service in the Borough and surrounding townships. Park personnel have been managing the bus contract for the Eisenhower NHS.

- Transit service could also be operated by an existing non-profit organization such as Main Street Gettysburg. Such an organization could be easily structured to represent all of the parties with an interest in the transit system. An existing non-profit organization would, however, have to obtain the technical expertise required to manage a transit system.

5.3 Method of Service Delivery

Service could be operated directly by a public agency or authority as described in the section above. However, since service is only needed seven months of the year, contracting all or part of the operation and maintenance to an existing transit operator has a number of advantages. This method is likely to provide the flexibility needed to adjust service levels based on demand. Contracting with private operators is the method used by some recent transit systems that have been implemented, including Bryce Canyon and Zion National Parks in Utah, Point Reyes National Seashore in California and Adams National Historic Park in Massachusetts. At Acadia National Park, service is operated by Downeast Transit, Inc., a private non-profit provider that has been providing demand-responsive service to local residents in the area for many years. The NPS has successfully contracted with Gettysburg Tours to provide service to the Eisenhower NHS, where service levels are varied significantly over the course of the year.

5.4 Vehicle Procurement

Vehicles procured need to be reliable, comfortable and easily recognizable. They should be operable in all weather conditions and provide heat, air-conditioning and windows that open to provide fresh air circulation. Gettysburg Tours currently operates historic, rubber-tired trolley service in Gettysburg and these vehicles fit well with the historic character of the area. While alternative fuel vehicles are desirable from an environmental standpoint, there are still concerns regarding liability, availability of alternate fuels, the infrastructure needed to fuel the vehicles and maintenance. Capital costs will also be higher than for diesel vehicles. Since reliability and high recognition are the most critical components for success of a new system, it is recommended that diesel-powered historic trolleys be considered for initial purchase.

5.5 Operations and Maintenance Funding

A number of Federal and State funding programs are available for capital equipment purchases but funds available for operations and maintenance are more limited. In order to sustain service over time, local sources of funding will need to be identified. Potential sources other than public funds include:

- **Fares** – Most urban transit systems charge patrons a fare to board the vehicle. This is less successful in recreational settings, where most visitors arrive in their cars and usually have free parking available. In addition, visitors tend to arrive in groups, and the cost of purchasing a ride for each person becomes expensive. Family passes are one method that can be used to mitigate this impact, but many parks have not been able to attract riders to voluntary systems that require a fare. Some parks in the fee demonstration program, including Adams NHS and Zion NP, have been able to incorporate the charge for use of the transit system into an entry fee. In addition, the Zion system is mandatory. Gettysburg is limited in this regard since the system will be voluntary and no entry fee is charged for the Park itself. Most of the revenue from the new Visitor Center attractions that will have an entry fee, such as the Cyclorama, are already dedicated to help pay for the construction of the Center itself.

- **Advertising** – While traditional advertising would not be appropriate in the Park itself, it could be used on Town routes and also on bus shelters located outside of the park, if tastefully done.

- **Contributions from Local Governments and Local Businesses** – Dedication of funds by both local governments and businesses is probably essential to the long-term success of the system. Business contributions can take a number of forms, including direct financial contribution, purchase of bus passes or tickets for customers, payment for direct door to door service and supply of in-kind services such as accounting, management or maintenance. Governmental agencies can offer in-kind services as well. Coordination between all of these entities provides the best opportunity for sustained funding.

5.6 Marketing and Promotion

Marketing and promotion of the system are critical to its success. While the new Visitor Center will serve as the focus of the promotional effort, it important that efforts be made to inform visitors of the availability of the system prior to their visit. Good signage must be provided on all major approach routes to inform visitors about the system. Signage within the Borough that is oriented to both drivers and pedestrians should also be provided. Traditional brochures with clear directions and instructions for using the system must be made widely available through the Visitor Center, motels, restaurants and other tourist and retail businesses. The Internet also offers great possibility to display schedules and information on services. Cross-promotion between the system and local businesses is also important. For example, riders can be given discount coupons for local businesses and businesses can be encouraged to advertise on the transit system's promotional materials and provide free or reduced-price bus passes to their customers. Other possible distribution channels include:

- Pennsylvania Welcome Centers;
- Internet including cross-promotion with business sites;
- Information included with hotel/motel reservations;
- Press release and/or advertising in Civil War or tourist-related publications; and
- Nearby tourist areas such as Lancaster and Washington, D.C.